W9-AIA-851

Animal World
THE SEAL

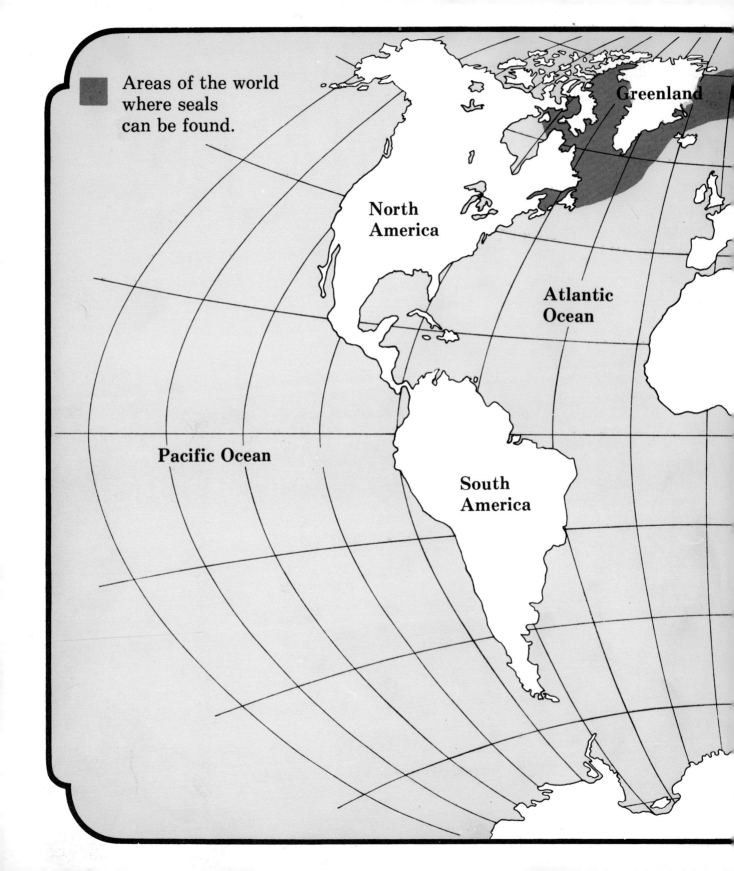

■ Areas of the world where seals can be found.

Greenland

North America

Atlantic Ocean

Pacific Ocean

South America

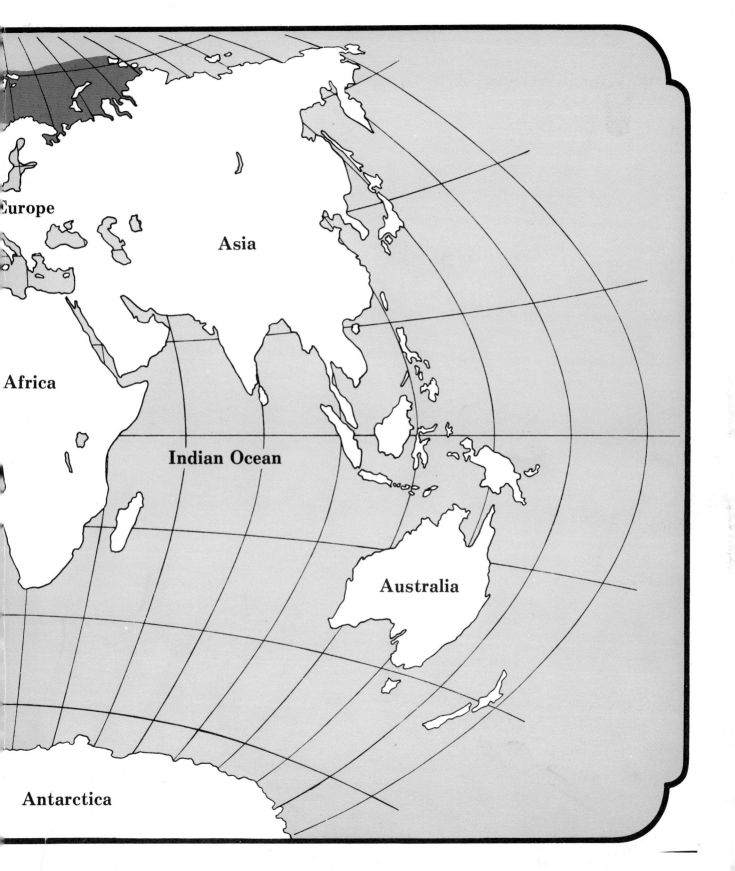

Europe

Asia

Africa

Indian Ocean

Australia

Antarctica

Published by The Rourke Enterprises, Inc., P.O. Box 711, Windermere, Florida 32786.
Copyright © 1983 by The Rourke Enterprises, Inc. All copyrights reserved. No part of this book may be reproduced in any form without written permission from the publisher. Printed in the United States of America.

Library of Congress Cataloging in Publication Data

Dalmais, Anne-Marie, 1954-
    My friend, the seal.

    (Animal world)
    Translation of: Mon ami, le phoque.
    Summary: Text and illustrations introduce the physical characteristics, habits, and natural environment of the seal.
    1. Seals (Animals) — Juvenile literature.   [1. Seals (Animals)]   I. Knox, Charlotte, ill.   II. Title.
III. Series.
QL737.P64D3413   1984   599.74'8   83-8993
ISBN 0-86592-867-3

Animal World
THE SEAL

illustrated by
Charlotte Knox

ROURKE ENTERPRISES, INC.
Windermere, FL 32786

The polar night

For three months the sun disappears completely from the Arctic polar region. This is the polar night.

A vast bluish shadow stretches over the enormous silent iceberg. The iceberg is a giant piece of ice. Almost unbroken, it extends from the North Pole to the Arctic Ocean.

This is the stunning scenery which awaits the seals.
    Tired of their underwater games, they have come to the surface to breathe the glacial air.

Spring—the birth of the baby seals

At last, the spring returns and the sun reappears. At first it shines for only a few hours a day. The rays warm the iceberg, which begins to come apart. Huge blocks of ice break off and drift away.

On sheltered and quiet territory, near the boundary of floating ice, the female seals gather. Here they give birth to babies which are already well developed and covered with beautiful white fur. The seals pictured here belong to a species which lives in Greenland.

Each mother seal takes very good care of her little one. She nurses it, protects it and feeds it with her milk, which is very rich.

First portrait

Let's look at this mother and baby. The young seal stays close to its mother and looks at the world through big, round eyes.

It has a fluffy, shiny coat of white fur. In about three weeks this coat will be replaced by a dense, rough one with grey speckles.

The seal's body is well adapted to arctic life. This baby does not freeze while lying on the ice. It is protected by a layer of fat. The fat keeps it warm. Later, that same fat will help it float on water with ease. Of course, this baby does not know how to swim yet.

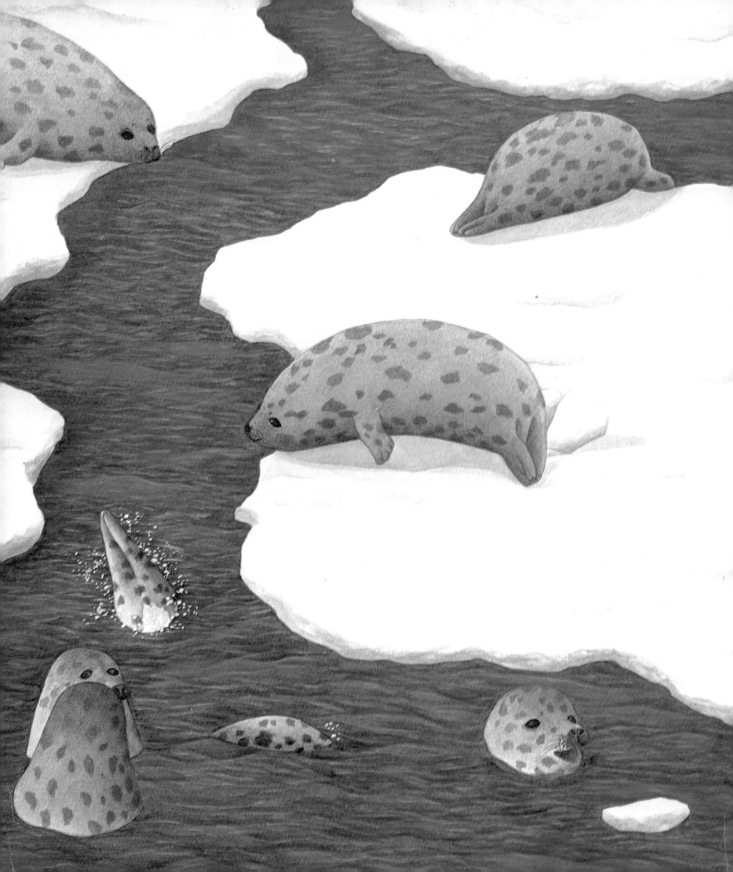

Swimming lessons

A few weeks have passed. The young seals have their new coats. They are no longer being watched by their mothers. They are big enough to be on their own.

Now it is time to practice swimming. Life in the water is very important to the seal. They dive, spin, leap and chase each other. They have a lot of fun, but this practice makes them stronger and better swimmers. They will develop great speed and flexibility. They will need these skills to capture food and to escape enemies.

On parade

Through exercise young seals become untiring swimmers. Now they want to show what they can do.

In this picture they have joined with a number of adults for an underwater tour. The flock includes a few large males with glistening yellow and grey fur patterned like a horseshoe.

Seals can stay underwater for twenty minutes. In this way, they have a lot of time to explore their world.

A meal on the run

Like all mammals, young seals drink their mothers' milk. It satisfies all their bodily requirements.

As they mature they will eat shellfish, such as shrimp and crab. Other favorites are cod, herring and salmon.

A full grown seal will need eleven pounds of fish a day. This sounds like a lot of food to be chasing every day. Actually, their speed and agility allow them to pursue schools of fish and catch them easily.

The enemies of the seal

Even during their games and chases, the seals must always be alert.
Powerful enemies lie in wait for them. Polar bears prowl around holes
in the ice waiting for seals to emerge from the water. In the water,
they must watch for sharks and killer whales.

   Of course, the worse enemy of the seals is man. Thousands of
newborn seals are massacred every year by seal hunters who sell their
beautiful fur.

From holes in the ice

The seasons pass. After spring comes an extraordinary summer. In summer the sun never sets. It is bright as daylight even in the middle of the night!

Soon enough, winter and darkness return. With the intense cold new ice is formed. Icebergs which split apart in spring are rejoined. They are floating "continents."

To keep from being trapped underneath, seals poke holes in the ice. Every so often they will emerge for a breath of fresh air.

Migrations

In spring the ice begins to melt. The schools of fish that are their food begin to migrate. Out of necessity, the seals migrate with them. They all move north in a procession which takes them past mountainous icebergs that sparkle in the sun.

SOME INTERESTING FACTS ABOUT SEALS

Species:

Seals belong to the species of mammals called "pinnipeds." Pinnipeg means "fin-footed." The front and hind limbs of the seal are really modified flippers. It is these flippers which give them flexibility and speed in the water. A swimming seal is a graceful thing to watch. On land, the flippers must be dragged behind the body, giving the seal an awkward, clumsy look.

There are eighteen varieties of seals. About nine of these live in the Arctic region. Five varieties live in the Antarctic and three live in the Pacific and Caribbean. Like their cousins, the walruses and sea lions, they prefer the colder climates.

All pinnipeds are carnivores. This means that they are meat eaters. In the case of seals, they prey on shrimp, crab, eel, herring and salmon. One of the largest variety of seals, the twelve foot long Leopard seal, will even pursue penguins and other seals.

Description:

The seal is beautifully designed for its watery home.

General body formation: Its body is tapered and streamlined. It can swim through water the way a bullet penetrates air. Seals are also expert divers. They are generally grey with markings.

Flippers: The front flippers are used for steering and the hind flippers propel the seal through the water.

Blubber: The body is surrounded by a layer of fat, called blubber. Blubber gives bouyancy and warmth in the icy ocean. It can also serve as a reserve food supply should fish become scarce.

Conservation:

Because seal fur is used to make expensive coats, the seal has been hunted for centuries. They use the same breeding grounds year after year so they are easy prey for hunters.

There is a group of islands southwest of Alaska called the Pribilof Islands. This is the breeding ground of the Northern Fur seal. These seals are greatly prized for their thick, soft fur.

Men have hunted seals on the Pribilof Islands for hundreds of years. Two hundred years ago there were five million seals. First came the Russians, then the Americans. By the early 1900's the seal population was down to one hundred thousand. The seals were in danger of extinction.

Conservationists worked long and hard to save these creatures. International treaties now protect the seals. The population has risen to one and a half million.

Eyes: Since seals have been known to dive three hundred feet in pursuit of prey, their eyes have adapted to seeing in the dark.

Nostrils: When the seal is underwater, the nostrils automatically close. Remember the seal is a mammal and cannot breathe underwater.

Teeth: Seals have sharp teeth, as do most meat eaters.

Ears: Many seals, like the harbor seal, have no outside ears. However, the fur seal, which is hunted for its skin, has tiny outside ears.

Size: The largest variety is the elephant seal. It is over twelve feet long. The Northern Fur seal can run eight feet long and seven hundred pounds. Harbor seals grow between four and six feet long and weigh one hundred to three hundred pounds.

Age: A well cared for seal in captivity will live about twenty years. In the wild the life expectancy is shorter.

Family Life:

Seals are sociable animals. They live in large herds or colonies. They take to land only for sleeping and breeding. Arctic seals gather on the edge of an iceberg. Seals in warmer climates rest on rocky places in a bay.

At breeding time the male (bull) stakes out his territory. He tries to attract as many females (cows) as possible. They are called a "harem." The bull will defend his harem and his territory from other bulls.

Seals are mammals. This means that the young are born live from their mothers, instead of in a shell. They are born with their eyes open, and covered with a beautiful coat of white fur. For at least a month they feed on their mothers' milk. Seal milk is very rich in fat. It is about thirteen times richer than cows' milk. With this diet, the baby grows quickly. In about a month he will be swimming. Seals love fun and games. During his childhood he will have a great time playing with all the other young seals.